Foreword

There are already several excellent books which chronicle the history of Leeds, providing the reader with an insight into how the modern city we know today functioned at the turn of the century.

Memories of Leeds is a collection of photographs that aim to capture and celebrate the nostalgia of an era that, for a great many people alive today, is very much within memory. For that reason, the period covered begins in the 1930s and progresses through the war years to the 1950s and 1960s.

Undoubtedly, as the new millennium approaches it is easier to look back on 'twentieth century Leeds' and see with some warmth many of the highlights of this great period of progress in our recent history.

The changes that have shaped our modern city centre are covered in a section in this book, and often present the reader with an opportunity to see streets and shopping areas that have either changed beyond recognition or disappeared altogether.

The Quarry Hill flats still have a place in the personal memories of many Leeds folk, and a selection of candid pictures capture the community feeling that the estate enjoyed in its earlier years. That piece of social experimentation is now largely thought to have been a mistake and, frankly, most Leeds people were pleased to have seen the back of them.

No book about the recent history of Leeds would be complete without reference to the sporting heritage of the city, so this book brings back memories of successes in the world of football, rugby and cricket. Sadly, we do not seem able to emulate that degree of success today!

I am a Leeds lad, born and bred, it is an immense honour for me to be the Lord Mayor of Leeds especially today, when our home city can proudly boast of our status as Capital of the North. To those of you who also like to remember yesterday, I say enjoy what lies inside this book.

Happy Memories.

M. J. Bedford

Lord Mayor of Leeds,
(Councillor Malcolm Bedford)
February 1997.

Some of the eager entrants to the Quarry Hill Estate Carnival fancy dress competition in July 1951.

First published in 1997 by:
True North Books
Dean Clough
Halifax
Tel 01422 344344
Printed by Joseph Ward ColourPrint,
Dewsbury. To Tom

a
true north
book

ISBN 1 900463 75X

£5.99 nett

Contents

City Square in the early 1930s. Then, as now, the hub of the city centre. The dome of the bank building on the right survives - sadly, the Royal Exchange building was replaced with an office block in the1960s.

Acknowledgments

The publishers would like to thank the following, whose help and co-operation have helped to make this book possible: Sandra Smith and all the staff at the Local and Family History section of Leeds Central Library; Bob Baldwin of Leeds United Football Club; Stuart Duffy, for his help in captioning the Leeds RLFC and Yorkshire County Cricket Club pictures; Mandy Walker for her expertise in designing the pages and Gareth Martin for organising the inclusion of the local companies profiled in this book. The publishers would also like to thank the mainly long established local companies who have supported this book by advertising with special thanks to the sponsors of the book, Wallace Arnold.

On her October 1958 visit to the city The Queen received a tremendously warm welcome, as can be seen in this picture taken on the shop floor of the Montague Burton Limited factory. Burtons employed 7000 workers in Leeds, with over three quarters of them being women. During the course of her visit The Queen took coffee in the factory's canteen, where the workers had an impromptu sing-song consisting of several verses of *Land of Hope and Glory* and *Rule Britannia*. The Chairman of Burtons, Mr Lionel Jacobson is shown escorting Her Royal Highness through the factory.

The 1958 Royal Visit is shown proceeding along The Headrow in this raised view. Thousands lined the route through the city centre, with bunting and Union Jacks visible along The Headrow and down towards Eastgate. The Queen was later to inspect a Guard of Honour at the Civic Hall. The days when people turned out in their thousands to see *any* member of the Royal family seem to belong to a different era to the one we live in today. Many historians explain this by pointing to the increase in popularity of television, which has brought such occasions into our living room. What is certain is that the occasion which exposed most ordinary people to television for the first time was the coronation of Queen Elizabeth in 1953 - the first constitutional event to be televised nationally.

Another Royal Visit, this time in October 1965. Many of the staff and even some of the patients at the General Infirmary had novel ideas on how to obtain a better view.

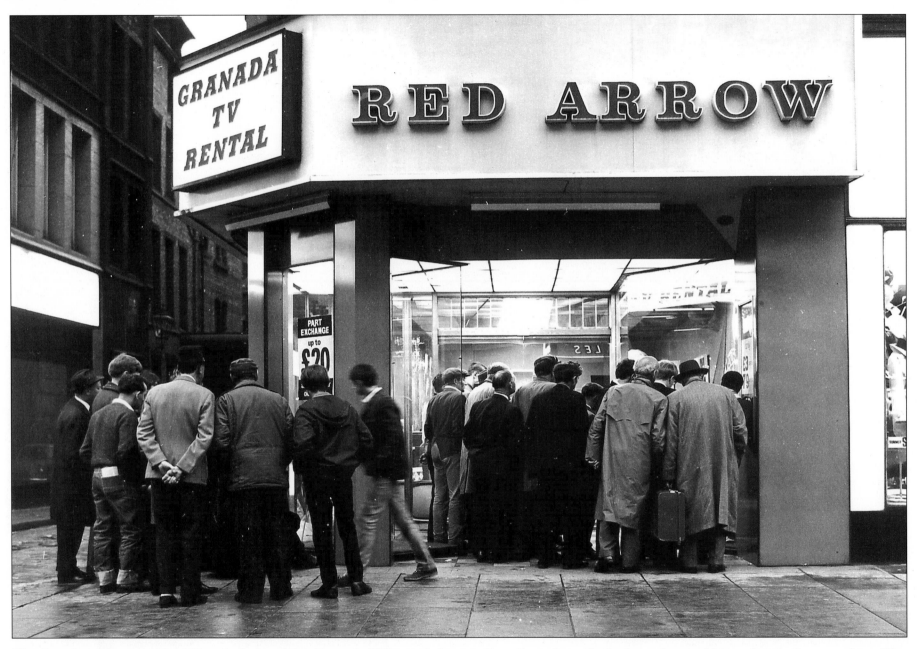

The fact that this crowd huddling in front of the Granada TV rental shop on Boar Lane is exclusively male provides a clue to the occasion. The date - July 1966 is an even better hint - the World Cup match was being played out at Wembley stadium, with the result about to be confirmed as English football's finest sporting triumph.

Quarry Hill Flats, pictured here under construction in 1938, were a social experiment in housing large numbers of people in what was then a completely untried type of dwelling. The origins of the scheme can be traced back to the "Houses of the Working Classes Act" of 1890, and the Quarry Hill site itself was formerly an area occupied by 2,800 slums and no fewer than 53 public houses. The blueprint for the project was to build a self-contained estate on a 26 acre site, three quarters of which was to be given over to open spaces and play areas. The method of construction employed, pioneered by Eugene Mapin, was also innovative in the way that a steel skeleton was erected onto which concrete panels were attached.

In total 939 family dwellings formed the Quarry Hill estate, housing nearly 2,500 people at its peak. The proximity of shopping and transport facilities to the estate was a part of the plan from the outset. Thus the logical place to site the city's new bus station was adjacent to the estate and the Markets area. Opened in August 1938 at a cost of £44,000, the bus station contained an air raid shelter for 150 people, reflecting the concern of the authorities at the increasing likelihood of war in Europe. The coming of war in 1939 did put a premature ending to some of the building work at Quarry Hill, with the work remaining unfinished some years after the war had ended.

Right: From the outset, the architect of the Quarry Hill estate, Mr RAH Livett, set out to create an environment that benefited from all the labour saving mod-cons available. One novel design feature was the "Garchey" system of waste disposal. Ashes and small items of refuse such as food tins were not put into dustbins, instead the Garchey sink fitted in each kitchen had a larger waste pipe into which the rubbish was dropped. On pulling a plunger, the waste would disappear into a network of pipes which eventually resulted in it being collected, dehydrated and then burnt. The system, which was said to be noiseless, did occasionally break down, on at least one occasion the city council had to rush out an emergency supply of dustbins to the estate!

Below: A typically well kept living room on the estate in October 1943. Unlike the high rise flats that were to follow in the 1960s, the flats at Quarry Hill were heated by coal.

Memories of Leeds

The pictures on this and the following pages capture the human face of Quarry Hill Flats. Although in its later years the estate attracted a poor reputation, there was a strong community spirit there in the 1940s and 50s, as these photographs show.

Left: Three chirpy young boys pose proudly for the camera. They were the page boys for the Estate's Carnival Queen in 1951, organised by the tenants association. The carnival was one of the social highlights on the estate and was held yearly in July. Alongside the carnival, the tenants association ran a Miss Teenage competition, which although centred around Quarry Hill estate, could be entered by any Leeds teenage girl. The 1951 competition attracted a £10 prize, presented by Lewis's and the Yorkshire Evening News. Miss Sheila Ainsworth, a 16 year old cashier, won the competition that year.

Below: Carnival Queen, Deidre Blackburn, aged 13, walks through the estate during the 1950 carnival, as a local photographer tries to take her picture. The carnival would begin with a procession around the estate in the morning and go on until 8.30pm with a programme of events taking place throughout the day.

Some of the young entrants to the 1951 Quarry Hill Estate carnival children's fancy dress competition sit in anticipation, with the backdrop of the flats behind them. Amazingly, 500 children entered the fancy dress competition that year. Looking at pictures like this, it is clear that, at least for a time, Quarry Hill enjoyed the kind of close community that its promoters had envisaged in the early 1930s. But even in 1951 problems were beginning to surface, with some people voicing their discontent through a BBC radio documentary based on the estate, produced in April of that year. The programme subsequently caused an uproar with many residents, when a fictional conversation in the programme described Quarry Hill as a 'dump'.

Closer inspection of this Quarry Hill carnival photograph provides a clue to the year. One of the boys is holding a coronation mug, suggesting 1953. The programme for the day's events each year was quite hectic, with games and competitions until late evening, usually finished off with a concert, performed by the children from the estate.

The final picture of Quarry Hill Flats belongs to a different time in the story of the estate. By the early 1970s the area had fallen into decay with the majority of its residents desperate to leave. The estate became much wider known when a television situation comedy, Queenie's Castle, was set there. The star of the show was Diana Dors, shown here in 1970. By this time, Quarry Hill's days were numbered, with the decision to demolish the estate coming in 1975. The bulldozers moved in the following year and by 1978 the final buildings had been flattened, thus drawing to a close perhaps one of the largest experiments in social housing Britain has seen this century.

Roberts Mart - a Leeds firm with family links that began in 1852.

In 1852 the founder of the company, William Roberts, commenced business as a paper merchant in Lady Lane, Leeds. Developments soon included hand made bag making, shortly followed by the acquisition of specialised machinery, progressing then into commercial printing. The premises have since been demolished. In 1875 the business was transferred to larger premises in Alfred Street which is situated off Boar Lane in the centre of Leeds. These premises have also been demolished.

In 1877 William Roberts died and the business was carried on for a time as William Roberts and Son by his widow and executors. At this time William Mart was taken into partnership having been employed as a traveller in Derby. The name of the firm was later changed to William Roberts, Son & Mart.

The name of the company was changed to Roberts, Mart & Co in 1888 and a warehouse was opened in Birmingham under the management of Walter Roberts.

In 1890 Roberts, Mart & Co Limited was formed as a private Limited Company, the board then consisted of John Roberts as chairman, with directors William Roberts and William Mart.

During 1891 the third portion of Bank Mills Estate was purchased and in 1892 the removal took place from Alfred Street to Bank Mills.

William Mart died in 1897 and the following year the remaining portion of the Bank Mills Estate was purchased and the extension of the building commenced, the portion which is still referred to as the New Mill being added.

Following the death of William Roberts in 1905 and John Roberts in 1924 Walter Roberts was then appointed chairman and managing director. In 1928 a decision was made to concentrate all production on Bank Mills, Leeds and the Birmingham warehouse was closed and an office opened at Martineau Street.

Above left: William Roberts, founder of the company that still bears his name.

Above: Women workers making paper bags by hand in 1916.

Left: This line drawing is of the premises of Roberts, Mart & Co. Ltd.

In 1947 Walter Roberts died and John Palliser Roberts, son of John Roberts and grandson of the founder, was appointed chairman and managing director. Two years later a sales office was opened in Sheffield. After John's death in 1954, the present chairman, Mr PK Roberts, became both chairman

and managing director and developments over the next 20 years included the manufacture and printing of cellulose film bags. On November 19th 1974, John Roberts, son of Mr PK Roberts, was appointed joint managing director.

During this period the main emphasis on sales involved supplying the retail trade with packaging materials, following the advent of the supermarket, the Company began to diversify into the merchanting of Polythene Bags and Carriers until 1977 when a four colour Italian Flexographic Printer was purchased, followed by continued investment in both bag making and printing equipment.

In July 1980, a 5,000 sq ft warehouse was built and in June 1983 Romar Packaging Limited was formed as a separate subsidiary company involved in the Extrusion and Conversion of Low Density Blown Film.

Since then, the company has continued to diversify. One of the main areas involved the household textile market and in July 1991, a patent was granted covering the manufacture of a Roll Pack Carrier Bag suitable for containing pillows and continental quilts.

The company's involvement in the food packaging industry since its inception has also been strengthened and the company currently supply major supermarkets with printed packaging for the overwrapping of products such as pork pies and sausages.

Continued investment involve the installation of an 8 colour Flexographic Printing Machine during 1991, accompanied by further additions of Polythene Converting Machines. In 1995 a second 8 Colour Flexographic Printing Machine was installed and a new Slitter rewinder.

The company still operates from Bank Mills. Romar Packaging Limited trades from Newmarket Lane and the present board of directors consists of Peter K Roberts as chairman, John Roberts as managing director, Peter Julian as sales director and Ken Ellis as financial director.

All the photographs date from September 30th, 1916 and are reproduced from the company photograph album.

Left: The Bookbinding department.

Below Left: A view of the lithographic machine room.

Below: The Letterpress machine department. Women were enlisted into the factories and mills, filling the spaces vacated by their husbands, sons and brothers.

Tetley's: The name for good beer and great pubs in Leeds

The Early Years

Mention the word Tetley's to most Leeds people and they will automatically think of the city's famous brewery, its beers, pubs, Shire horses or award winning visitor centre.

Tetley's and Leeds have been synonymous almost from the time Joshua Tetley, a maltster from Armley, bought the brewery from his friend and maltings customer, William Sykes, in October 1822.

Expansion

As the Tetley brewery expanded in the last century so the Tetley family decided to buy their own pubs. The first one they purchased, The Duke William in Bowman Lane, is now in the brewery yard. Bought in July 1890, the pub closed in the 1950s to become the brewery's first medical centre.

The second pub Tetley's bought was The Fleece, Town Street, Farsley. This pub is still open today and proudly bears a plaque recording its important place in the history of the company.

Tetley's Brewery Wharf

It wasn't until research was done for a book on the history of Tetley's in the early 1980s that the historical significance of The Duke William was realised.

The pub - which became part of the brewery as the original site expanded - now forms part of the Tetley's Brewery Wharf visitor centre attraction, which opened in Easter 1994.

Left: An early advertiser on the city's trams, Tetley's often shared advertising space with another famous Leeds Brewery, Melbourne, which merged with Tetley's in 1960.

This photograph of the Original Oak, Headingley, records the visit to Leeds of Her Majesty, The Queen on 22nd October 1965. The Royal procession passed this landmark pub - which has been Tetley's most successful pub for many years - after the Queen officially opened Seacroft's Town Centre development.

Tetley Strength

Since September 1995, all Tetley pubs have become part of a national pub operating company, Allied Domecq Inns, which is part of Allied Domecq Retailing, a division of the international company, Allied Domecq plc.

The Tetley brewery is part of Carlsberg-Tetley, the third largest brewery company in the UK, who provide their beers to Allied Domecq Retailing, other pub operating companies, free houses and clubs.

However, such is the strength of the Tetley name in the north of England almost a thousand Allied Domecq Inns pubs are still signed Tetley's and licensees, staff and customers continue to play their part in the local community under the sign of the Huntsman.

Pub Appeal

These pubs pride themselves on offering places to relax, talk, enjoy hand pulled beers, listen to music, play pool alongside more traditional games like darts, raise money for local good causes, offer something to eat, share a joke, read a newspaper, catch up with the local gossip ... the list seems endless.

In today's ever stressful world the appeal of the pub remains timeless.

Styles and living standards may have changed over the years but a Tetley's local provides customers with a true glimpse of what pub culture is all about in the North of England.

Above: Being so close to the Headingley headquarters of Yorkshire County Cricket Club and Leeds Rugby League, the Three Horse Shoes on Otley Road has always appealed to supporters of both sports.

Left: This photograph of The Templar in Vicar Lane was taken soon after the pub's previous owners, Ind Coope, merged with Tetley's in 1961.

Every plumbing and heating fitting you could ever need...

IMI Yorkshire Fittings Limited has been working with copper and its alloys for over one hundred years. From their head office in Stourton, Leeds, they have developed their range of fittings and valves to such a degree that now they are widely regarded as amongst the best engineered products of their kind.

From Racecourse to Factory

The first industrial use of the Stourton site dates from 1888 when Elmore's Depositing Co. manufactured copper tubes there. However, in the early 1880s the site was actually a racecourse and the venue for the St. Ledger.

The Yorkshire connection began in 1909 when Elmore's became the Yorkshire Copper Works (YCW), producing high quality condenser tubing.

The War Years

The advent of the First World War saw a break in tube production when the company was requisitioned to manufacture munitions for the war effort. Most manufacturing companies faced the same hardships at that time, with the Government turning many industries over to the more pressing need for armaments. The Great War also saw an influx of women workers, brought in to carry out what was often hard physical work in place of their husbands, sons and brothers.

Left: A section from one of the first Yorkshire Copper Works advertising brochures. The drawing shows the works in about 1906/7.

Below: The same site, dating from the 1940s.

The late Duke of Kent visiting the Yorkshire Copper Works during his tour of Leeds factories on 27th May, 1931. The Duke is seen fourth from the left, looking down lengths of copper piping which was subsequently turned into the plumbing fittings that are now world renowned. During the 1930s Britain suffered from the worst depression it had ever experienced but despite this, the Yorkshire Copper Works was still able to expand. This can partly be explained by the inter-war house building programme that saw both local government and private developers expand into suburbia to build the new model housing estates.

The capillary fitting for light gauge copper tube

YORKSHIRE IMPERIAL

YORKSHIRE IMPERIAL METALS LIMITED
HEAD OFFICE: P.O. BOX 166, LEEDS

ICI Merger

However, by the 1920s normal production had resumed and, from the 1930s, business boomed as copper enjoyed widespread growth in domestic plumbing systems. In the period following the launch of its mow famous Yorkshire integral solder ring fitting in 1934, the Yorkshire Copper Works was so successful that in 1958 it merged with the ICI Metals Division to become known as Yorkshire Imperial Metals (YIM).

IMI Yorkshire Fittings

In 1968, Yorkshire Imperial Metals was incorporated into the Building Products Group of IMI plc, a major international industrial group and in 1986 took on its present identity and the name IMI Yorkshire Fittings Limited.

Since then, the company has developed from being one with a largely UK focus to a major European supplier with manufacturing, sales and distribution operations throughout Europe, servicing domestic and export markets all over the world.

Over the past one hundred years, accumulated experience of working with copper to develop solutions for pipework system designers and installers has given IMI Yorkshire Fittings the expertise to manufacture the highest quality products for industrial and domestic users throughout the world.

Together with Kuterlite compression fittings, Endex end feed fittings, Tectite push-fit fittings and the Yorkshire integral solder ring fittings ensure IMI Yorkshire Fittings has the products for every conceivable plumbing and heating application.

Left: This picture dating from March 1965 shows the front cover of the company brochure.
Below: The inside front cover of the same brochure, describing the novel way in which the capillary action of the solder creates the perfect seal.

For nearly 30 years 'Yorkshire' Fittings have been recognised as the foremost of capillary fittings providing the neatest and most efficient method of jointing light gauge copper tube.
Made to the requirements of B.S. 864 they are fabricated in Copper, Brass or Gunmetal and are designed for use with tubes to B.S. 659, particulars of which are given on page 3.

The 'Yorkshire' Fitting utilizes the principle of capillary attraction and incorporates as an integral part (located in a groove formed in the wall of the socket) the correct amount of solder for making a perfect joint.

Correct size tubes and fittings are used together, the surfaces to be joined are cleaned, properly fluxed, assembled together and then heated. This is all that is necessary for making satisfactory joints. When the solder becomes molten with the heat applied it runs from the groove in which it is located between the surfaces of the tube and fitting and its appearance at the mouth in a complete ring is proof of a sound joint.

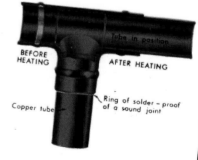

BEFORE HEATING
AFTER HEATING
Tube in position
Copper tube
Ring of solder - proof of a sound joint

This aerial view of the Yorkshire Copper Works dates from the 1960s. The photograph was taken from roughly the same place as the earlier line drawing of the site. The River Aire can be seen clearly running down the right side of both pictures.

Berwin & Berwin: Quality Clothing for almost a Century

Founder Barnett Berlyn

The story of one of the country's foremost independent clothing manufacturers began almost a century ago in Bobruisk, a village in White Russia.

Barnett Berlyn, a young tailor, decided that the only way to escape the oppression and poverty of his homeland was to emigrate to England and seek a better living. This meant temporarily leaving his wife, Sara and four children - Betsy, Louis, Ted and another child, behind when he sailed for England, destined for the city of Leeds - then, as now the centre of the tailoring industry in Britain.

Arriving in Leeds, Barnett soon found work with John Barron, the large suit manufacturer who employed many Jewish immigrants. Having found employment, Barnett sent for his family, who were to endure a harrowing journey so dangerous that, tragically, the youngest child died on the trip.

The family set up home in Trafalgar Street, part of an area known as the Leylands. Conditions were appaling, with poor sanitation and overcrowding - hard to face for people who had come from rural areas. Barnett and Sara saw their family grow in the following years after the arrival of two daughters, Leah and Joan and a son, Jack. Eventually the family were able to improve their lot and move to Coburg Street, an area which is now occupied by the Merrion Centre. Sons Louis and Ted trained as tailors, following in the footsteps of their father. Jack trained as a cutter.

Barnett became a foreman for John Barron and by about 1920 set up on his own. Joined by Louis and working from Coburg Street, this was the beginning of the Berwin business. Ted joined his father and brother and took on the role of salesman, making his first call to Barrow in Furness were he persuaded a retailer to give the fledgling business some work. Further business soon followed from other northern towns as a result of Ted's sales trips which were then by rail, the large baskets (skips) of samples being carried by porters.

Soon the business was making suits, jackets and, in particular, raincoats - which were becoming an increasingly successful line, with larger premises in Bridge Street necessary to accommodate the extra trade.

In the early 1930s the firm continued to prosper and the sales of raincoats grew even further, enabling the business to acquire additional premises in St. Peters Building, opposite what is now the main city centre bus station. Around this time the business suffered a major setback when a large customer in London went into liquidation, leaving a considerable amount owing. So stung were they by this act that the brothers said they would never trade with a London based company again. This policy remained until the early 1960s but has now totally changed.

Before the business became a limited company in 1933, the family name was changed to Berwin in response to the prejudice that the name Berlyn had attracted in the aftermath of the First World War. By 1935 the company had grown sufficiently to relocate its two separate sites under one roof when the factory at Roseville Road was acquired. Sadly, Barnett Berwin died before he could see the new premises occupied.

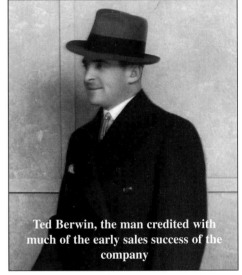

Ted Berwin, the man credited with much of the early sales success of the company

Despite the nationwide slump of the 1930s, business continued to be buoyant for the company, with Louis taking charge of production, Ted, sales and Jack, accounts and administration.

The dawning of hostilities in 1939 saw many changes to the business, with part of the factory being requisitioned by the government and given over to another company whose factory had been used for war work.

master tailored by Berwin

Left: A price list for made to measure tailoring from 1962.

Right: A late 1950s advertisement for raincoats, a major part of the company's product range at the time, thanks to their popularity with buyers.

Many local companies found their production being directed to support the war effort. This was also the case with B. Berwin Ltd, who were given the prestigious contract for the production of American officers uniforms. By the end of the war the factory was released back into the possession of the company and Louis's son, Malcolm Berwin, who was studying at Leeds University, was given the job of redesigning the new layout for the works.

The post war years saw business again prosper, with a new factory acquired at Westland Road, off Dewsbury Road for the production exclusively of raincoats. Soon after this Malcolm Berwin joined the business after national service and graduating from university. As the decade moved on, the Korean War caused raw materials prices for many businesses to soar and brought on a recession, which affected the clothing industry particularly badly. Owing to this it took two years before the new factory would be fully occupied.

The 1960s saw Berwin & Berwin continue to grow and enjoy good profit margins, employing 300 staff by the middle of the decade. Louis Berwin died in 1964 and Malcolm became a director. By the end of the decade the firm had three sites and running these separately was becoming difficult, so in 1971 the Roseville Road factory was bought out of the proceeds of the previous premises. Moving the entire operation to the new site took just two weekends, without any disruption to production. In 1973 Malcolm's son, Simon, the fourth generation of the family, joined the company.

More recently the company trebled its size when it acquired the "long run" factory at South Kirby near Pontefract. This enabled Berwin & Berwin to provide an even better service to High Street retailers, who require higher volumes of suits, jackets and coats. The Leeds factory is still geared towards producing shorter runs of very high quality tailoring, with customers such as Harrods, Austin Reed and Burberry to its credit. Just prior to the acquisition of the new factory the company was honoured by the visit of the Princess Royal to mark the 50th anniversary of the business.

Malcolm Berwin continues to take an active role in the company as President, with his son Simon in day-to-day charge as Managing Director. Edward Stanners, an old family friend, became Chairman in 1991. Financial Director, Bill Hodgson has completed 20 years at the company, the Production Director, Philip Harris starting his working life there, a reflection on the loyalty of many Berwin & Berwin employees. Indeed one employee, Roy Farrar, has spent over 51 years at the company, with one family clocking up 150 years between three of its members who all worked there.

As well as serving the home market Berwin & Berwin are very proud of their export success, with 20% of the Leeds factory's production going abroad. This achievement was officially recognised in 1994 when Princess Anne, the Princess Royal, presented the British Clothing Export Council Menswear Award for Export Achievement to the company.

Today Berwin & Berwin employs 700 people, more than double the number of 30 years ago, and is the largest independent clothing manufacturer in the country. Almost a century after Barnett Berwin began as a tailor in Leeds, the fourth generation of his family look to the next millennium, confident that, with their managers and staff, the future for Berwin & Berwin will be even better than the past.

Over 140 years of success that began with one man and his idea

There are few centres of industry in the United Kingdom that can compare with Leeds in the number and variety of manufacturers and enterprise of its inhabitants. Prominent among the large establishments is Pickersgill Kaye at Hunslet. Established in 1855 by Joseph Kaye as a small engineering concern, the original business was primarily oil can manufacture. The company was originally based at Horsforth in Leeds but twelve years later, demand for their products saw a necessity for bigger premises and after becoming incorporated during 1867 they moved to South Accommodation Road, at Hunslet in Leeds.

The company continued to diversify over

All the photographs on this page date from the mid 1920s. **Above:** *The original outlet for the products of Joseph Kaye Ltd, a small shop in High Holborn, London.* **Left and below:** *Like many businesses around the time of the First World War, a good many of the workers at Joseph Kaye were women. Incredibly, forty railway companies bought their door locks from the company.*

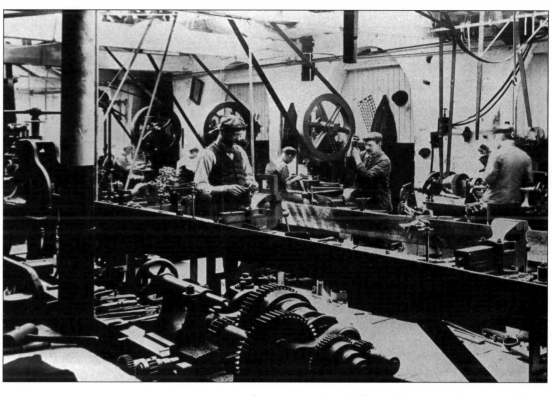

the following years, eventually specialising in lock manufacture. Their list of clients bears weight to their exceptional ability to supply quality products. No less than forty customers, all of them railway companies, were supplied with Kaye's Patent Locks during the first half of this century. Door Locks, handles and knobs, finger plates and lavatory 'Engaged' locks were amongst the many varying products of that time.

In 1953 a young man by the name of Harry Pickersgill set up a Jig & Tool design business, supplying Kaye's with tooling designs. Fourteen years later Harry and his son, David formed a partnership to design and manufacture tooling in Horsforth, Leeds. They employed four people. Three years later the assets of Joseph Kaye Ltd were purchased by Pickersgills and Pickersgill - Kaye was incorporated. The company employed seventeen people in Horsforth and twenty of the staff of Joseph Kaye in Hunslet. The following year all employees were moved to the South Accommodation site in Hunslet.

In 1980 the company moved to its present site at Pepper Road, when the council purchased the land on which the site stood.
Two years later the recession forced the redundancy of 54 employees but during that same year, two sister companies were formed: PK Tooling and Pickersgill Electroplating Ltd.

Pickersgill-Kaye went from strength to strength following this move and by 1989 they employed 120 people and became a holding company. Nowadays the company employs more than 150 employees, a long way from its humble beginnings of only four.

Above and below left: More photographs dating from the 1920s.

Above Left: Mr Joseph Kaye, founder of the company. During his youth he worked in a mill at Beeston Royds where he invented a setting-on motion for spinning mules which was used for many years. He took out many patents during his life, and Kaye's oil cans and locks were, and still are, known all over the world. His wife suggested the idea for a fare-bow on trams and her name, as well as that of her husband's is on the original patent. Mr Kaye died in 1902 aged 77 years.

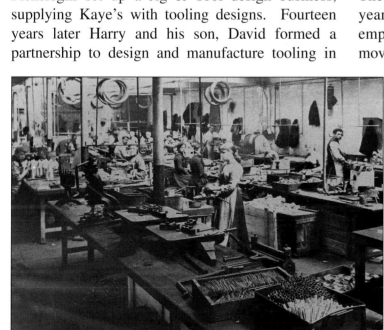

Almost a century of serving the Leeds electrical industry

William Hargreaves, father of the first MD whose collieries were the main customer in the early years.

Scattergood and Johnson was founded almost a century ago by Bernard P Scattergood who was previously an electrical engineer with Marshall & Fowler. It was four years later when Claude Johnson joined as partner. Mr Johnson remained with the company for only two years, yet his name remains to this day.

In 1912 JN Hargreaves joined his small business to that of Scattergood and Johnsons' and the company was moved to 7-9 Cookridge Street & Alexandra Street.

Mr Hargreaves' brother was involved with local collieries and Scattergood & Johnson supplied them with all their electrical equipment including Reyrolle plugs and sockets. The company developed and was incorporated in 1924 at which time JN Hargreaves became managing director.

In 1937 Bernard Scattergood died, leaving a bequest to Queen's College, Oxford, to assist the sons of graduates of Oxford and Cambridge, whereby parents of limited means may be assisted to give their children a University education.

Three years after the war, JN Hargreaves' son, Christopher joined the company after serving a four year electricians apprenticeship in Peckfield Colliery.

During that year the pits were nationalised and Scattergood and Johnson suffered a staggering blow, losing 90% of their business almost overnight.

The next five years were an uphill struggle, having to rebuild the business from the ashes of the pit nationalisation but in 1953 they were appointed English Electric Distributor, providing the cornerstone of the power and distribution business. The following year Christopher became managing director and the business moved again in 1956, to 30-31 St. Paul's Street and five years later the company was appointed stockists for MTE Motor Control Gear and once again they felt the need to move, transporting the business to 37 - 39 St Paul's

Street, a little further along the road, in much bigger premises.

Christopher soon became chairman of the company, gaining complete control, and there followed another move in 1966 to Lowfields Road. Three years later his father died and there followed a period of change, seeing first, Joe Wardell and later, George Beaumont appointed to the board.

In 1972 a franchise was obtained for Allen Bradley products - now the base of the automation business. In 1982 a branch of Scattergood and Johnson was opened in Sheffield, following a calm period of good profit and growth. Nowadays, Scattergood and Johnson have branches in Gateshead, Manchester and Sheffield as well as the head office at Lowfields Road in Leeds.

Still privately owned, the company has expanded rapidly over the last ten years and although their reputation for quality and service remains undiminished, they have rationalised their suppliers to only the top brand names, offering their customers more than 25,000 high quality stock lines at competitive prices. Contributing to the company's success throughout the years has been their insistence on offering customers exactly what they want.

Facing Page, Far Left: This certificate dates from 1932 and shows the appointment of S & J as a CMA Authorised Factor to the Cable Makers Association.
Main Picture, facing page: The Saint Paul's Street shop taken during the mid 1950s.
Below left: Another view of the Saint Paul's Street works.
Below: An interior shot of the showroom in the late 1960s showing some of the popular products of the day.

Lax & Shaw: A commitment to excellence in glass manufacturing

Lax & Shaw Ltd was established in Hunslet, Leeds in 1891 by Thomas Lax and John Shaw and was primarily involved with the manufacture of handmade pharmaceutical containers.

The current site at South Accommodation Road was acquired in 1928. Up until 1938 the company operated several different factories, called Albert Works,

Co-founder Lax & Shaw, Thomas Lax

Belinda Works, Clarence Works and Donisthorpe Works, taking the first four letters of the alphabet. The company had the reputation of being the country's top supplier of baby feeding bottles and had the telegram address of Feeders, Leeds. Ten years later, a period of consolidation began with the closure of Albert Works and the building of the third furnace at the present site. Four years later saw the closure of Clarence Works.

Expansion continued at the South Accommodation site until, in 1964, the first Independent Section Machine was installed, signalling a major change in glass manufacturing methods. By the late 1970s all the semi-automatic machines had been replaced. Lax & Shaw was bought by Associated British Foods in the mid 60s, with Mr Gerald Shaw, the

founder's grandson, continuing as managing director until his retirement in 1987.

The company rationalised its operations and invested heavily in the 1980s to the tune of £15 million. With the recession severely affecting glass sales in the early 80s and the increasing popularity of plastic bottles, it was decided to shut down one furnace, rationalise facilities by investing heavily in new technology and reappraise the potential market.

It was clear that the container industry was facing a major rationalisation programme, just as had happened in other glass-producing companies. The need for low cost production in higher volume areas meant that the major container companies had to invest heavily in larger, faster and more cost effective machines. It was certain that this would have the effect of polarising producers away from 'all things to all markets' towards high volume, highly flexible production on the other.

With less than 2% of the UK capability at that time, Lax & Shaw had no pretensions to be involved with the high volume market, and therefore targeted highly flexible equipment and methods to address the niche market which it now serves. The liquor industry was seen as an ideal target market, demanding specially designed bottles in low volumes and a good mix of medium volume products suitable for the same types of machine.

At high risk, Lax & Shaw took on the world's first license of Vapocure, a special process to colour coat glass. The production plant was installed in 1987 and further investment in colour coating was made in a second, more flexible line in 1992.

With the success of the marketing strategy, along with the Colouring processes and resurgence of glass as a high quality packing medium, thanks in part to the Green movement, the company made the decision in 1989 to invest in a further production plant which included a new 170 ton furnace, raw materials plant and hot and cold end equipment.

In addition a new CAD/CAM draughting system was installed, which dramatically shortened the lead time from design concept to glass, even enabling customers to develop ideas on screen and produce models.

With the expansion of activities in Leeds, a Scottish sales office was opened in Falkirk in 1989. The decision to set up in Scotland was an important one, considering that almost 65% of the company's production for the liquor market is shipped to Scotland for filling. Lax & Shaw's centenary was celebrated on 4th September 1991, 100 years to the day that Thomas Lax paid the deposit on the Albert Works.

The company continues to develop and aims to achieve a £40 million turnover by the year 2000. This will be attained through continued investment by parent company ABF Plc, market and product diversification and commitment to its employees.

Left: A group of engineers at Lax & Shaw during the Second World War years.

Above: This photograph, dating from a slightly earlier period shows a group of cloth capped workers sat with a horse drawn cart, a usual form of transport for that time.

Large picture - facing page: Schiller Semi automatic machines in operation at Clarence Works in the early 1930s.

The impact of wartime is striking in this photograph of The Headrow, taken during 1942. Virtually every aspect of life in city centre Leeds was affected. Aside from the large number of uniformed servicemen visible, the most obvious physical evidence of wartime precautions are the civil defence water tanks sited in the middle of the road, there in case of incendiary bomb attacks by air raid. There are also large brick bomb blast barriers built in front of the entrance to Lewis's, which would have protected the people inside to some extent should The Headrow have come under attack. The lamp standards down The Headrow had the bulbs removed throughout the war years as a blackout measure.

The Home Guard, affectionately known as "Dad's Army" to many, played an increasingly significant part in the country's civil defence measures as the war progressed. In Leeds, members of the Home Guard found themselves guarding prisoners of war, as well as manning the anti-aircraft guns situated at Adel and Knostrop.

Leeds suffered relatively little from air raids compared to many other northern cities - some said because the layer of smog from the city's many mill chimneys provided an ideal smoke screen! However, the Town Hall was bombed in March 1941, suffering substantial damage. The following year Winston Churchill made an unscheduled stopover in the city, and despite the fact that only two hours notice of his visit was given, some 20,000 people came to hear him speak on the Town Hall steps.

Above: Members of the Home Guard on target practice in Bramley.

Left: Not the result of a real air raid, but certainly realistic enough. Leeds Home Guard members practice searching through debris for survivors. "Bodies" made out of sacks and old rags were hidden in the wreckage in order to make the exercise as close to reality as possible. This picture was taken in the Kirkstall area.

Few would argue that the years from the mid 1960s to the late 1970s were the greatest on record for Leeds United. This picture dates from July 1964, a time when the fortunes of the club were beginning to advance in leaps and bounds. Led by the legendary Don Revie ,the previous season had seen the club gain promotion from the old Second Division, and the end of the 64/65 season resulted in Leeds being runners up in what was then the top division of British soccer. Pictured (Left to right) are back row: Willie Bell, Paul Reaney, Freddie Goodwin, Gary Sprake, Brian Williamson, Norman Hunter, Ian Lawson, Front row: Johnny Giles, Billy Bremner, Jim Storrie, Bobby Collins, Don Revie, Don Weston, Jimmy Greenhoff, Jack Charlton.

Like most towns and cities across the North, the city of Leeds has enjoyed sporting success on the rugby league field as well as soccer. The Leeds Rugby League football team from 1965 are pictured here at Headingley: Back Row (Left to right): "Budgie" Firth, Mick Clark, Allan Lockwood, John Sykes, Dick Gemmell, Louis Neuman, Drew Broatch. Front Row: Mick Shoebottom, Ken Rollin, Les Chamberlain, Ronnie Cowan, Geoff Wrigglesworth, Robin Dewhirst.

Memories of Leeds

Above: One of Leeds' less obvious sporting heroes is pictured here in September 1967, presenting medals to some of Jack Lane Athletic Club's up and coming wrestlers. Jimmy Savile, later to become Sir Jimmy Savile OBE, was himself an accomplished semi-professional wrestler before his meteoric rise to fame as a radio and later TV presenter.

Below: Headingley has been the home of Yorkshire County Cricket since the county game began. Here, the Yorkshire team are pictured at another piece of history that has all but disappeared - Bradford Park Avenue Ground with the old football stand in the background. The picture dates from 1969.

Pictured are, back row left to right: Chris Balderstone, John Hampshire, Tony Nicholson, Richard Hutton, Chris Old, Geoff Boycott, Geoff Cope. Front row: Phil Sharpe, Jimmy Binks, Brian Close, Doug Padget, Don Wilson.

Memories of Leeds

Right: England and Leeds players Norman Hunter and Jack Charlton receive some well-earned adulation on the steps of the Civic Hall in July 1966, after returning to Leeds after the World Cup victory. They were later to attend a civic reception hosted by the Lord Mayor.

Left: Perhaps two of the best known sporting figures that have been at Elland Road over the years, Don Revie and Billy Bremner pose for this 1970 photograph. The occasion was a great double for the famous pair when Revie was awarded the Bell's Trophy for Manager of the Year and Bremner won the coveted Football Writers Association Player of the Year.

Changing City Centre

Two pictures capture a glimpse of 1930s life around City Square. Then, as now, very much the hub of the city, the Square itself was created at the turn of the century, very much the vision of Col. W T Harding, Lord Mayor of Leeds, 1898-99. The large picture is dominated by the Royal Exchange building, which was demolished and replaced with an office block in the 1960s. The inset picture shows the war memorial, sited after the Great War in City Square at a cost of £5,000. As road traffic increased in subsequent years the Cenotaph was moved to its present site on The Headrow.

This view from City Square was probably taken from the Royal Exchange building and provides a good elevated view of Infirmary Street. Even in the 1930s when the number of vehicles was a fraction of those on the road today, the traffic congestion in City Square was quite considerable. The Standard Life Assurance building is the main focal point of this view, with its impressive architecture. In the redevelopment boom that followed in the 1960s this building was knocked down to be replaced by the Norwich Union office block, which has itself recently been demolished to make way for a new building, the appearance of which is, arguably, an improvement on its predecessor.

Motor buses and trams all conspire to provide this busy scene in City Square during the early 1930s. Trams were first used in Leeds in 1874 and many city centre tram tracks were subsequently relaid at the turn of the century, using wooden blocks rather than the usual stone setts to reduce noise levels. Leeds trams were to continue in operation many years after other town and cities. It is, perhaps, ironic that in recent year cities like Manchester and Sheffield have invested millions in setting up city centre tram networks - lending weight to the saying that "there is nothing new under the sun!".

Leeds City Station opened for business in 1846 on the site that it still occupies to this day. Initially operated by the Leeds and Bradford Railway Co. Ltd., it was taken over by the Midland Railway Company in 1852. The Queen's Hotel is seen here in the early stages of construction in 1936. Opened by the Earl of Harewood in March 1937, its facade is still as impressive today as it was back then. The course of the main line through Leeds has served to divide the city centre into two halves, the northerly of which housing shops and offices, with the area to the south of the line mainly occupied by industry. Evidence of this can be seen by the number of mills and chimneys visible in the distance of this view.

This more recent view of City Square is from the early 1950s. The tram and bus shelters are visible, as is the entrance to the underground lavatories, where a hot bath was also available. When the Square was redeveloped around a decade after this photograph was taken, it was decided that the toilets were no longer required so, rather than demolish them, they were merely covered over. Presumably, they still exist as a type of lavatorial time capsule beneath the City Square of today!

1930s Briggate, looking up towards the Headrow. At first glance the streets appear to be empty, but a closer look will reveal the ghostly images of people walking up and down the street. This is caused by the long aperture setting that the early photographer needed to get his shot. Montague Burton enjoys a prominent frontage further down on the left hand side of Briggate, known then as *"The Tailor of Taste"*. Basil Rathbone topped the bill at the Rialto cinema. Assuming that the clock in the foreground is correct, this was an early morning photograph.

Left: Frank Winfield Woolworth's Briggate store was undergoing an extension in this wartime picture. The first Woolworths opened in Liverpool in 1904 and the familiar 3d and 6d stores were soon in virtually every town and city across the country. The posters on the wooden boarding carry typical wartime messages. Air raids were a constant threat in larger industrial town and cities.

Right: Taken by the City Engineers, this view of The Headrow was intended to be used to consider the resiting of the war memorial, which was still in City Square when this picture was taken. The war memorial was later moved to the Headrow, where it still stands today.

Right: It would be fairly unlikely today to find a car showroom in the middle of a city centre, particularly with the premium rates applicable to such areas, but in 1935 when this picture was taken there was a *Standard Cars* dealer on Albion Street. Standard cars were later to become part of the Triumph motor company.

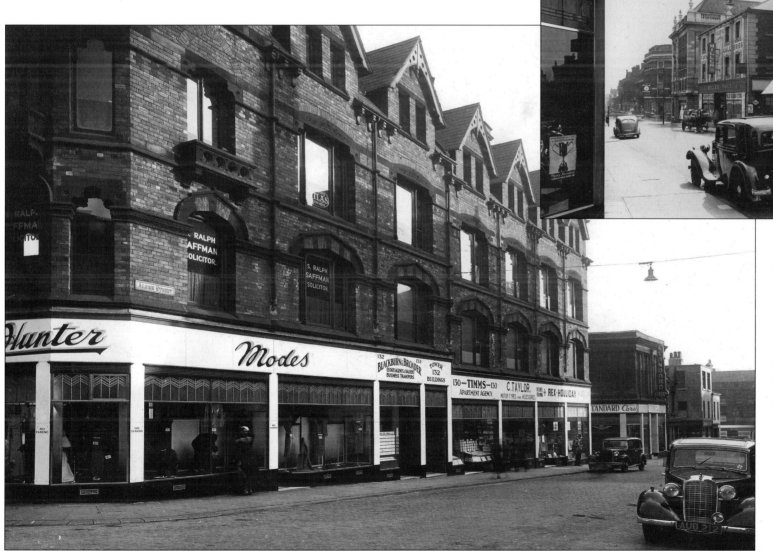

Left: The window display at Modes clothiers attracts a passing window shopper.

Albion Street, running from Merrion Street at the northern extreme of the city centre to Boar Lane at the southernmost, is a busy and prosperous part of the city centre. These two pictures date from the 1930s and show the area before much of the lower part was closed to traffic.

April 1951 in Briggate, with the street almost overflowing with shoppers, trams and cars. The police telephone box in the foreground was one of several sited throughout the city centre in the days before police radios. The site of so many trams was common in Leeds but unusual in most other towns and cities, who had mostly scrapped their tram networks before the war, with the motor bus usually taking their place.

Rationing was still in place in the post war years and although this and the general economic difficulties facing the country in the immediate aftermath of the war meant trade was generally slow, crowds were still common in Briggate.

Right: Lands Lane is today right in the hub of the city centre shopping area, adjacent to Schofields. The buildings shown here in 1967 are, in fact right opposite what was until recently called the Schofield's Centre. The Queen's Arcade remains a popular shopping venue, linking Lands Lane with Briggate. The presence of the Ford Zephyr on Lands Lane confirms that this picture was taken before the street was pedestrianised.

Left: Albion Street, also taken in 1967. The lower end of Albion Street was affected by redevelopment much more so than this area, with the building of the Bond Street centre (since renamed Leeds Shopping Plaza) and the creation of two large multi-storey car parks.

An early 1960s view of The Post Office at City Square taken from the small traffic island that divides the main traffic from the area in front of the Queen's Hotel. The most obvious difference about the traffic compared with today is that City Square had a two-way system, unlike the one way "loop" which was introduced in the 1970s. The Post Office was built in 1896-98, flanked in this view by the Standard Life Assurance building which was demolished soon after this picture was taken, to be replaced by the Norwich Union tower, itself recently flattened after a lifetime of less than thirty years.

Close inspection of this early 1960s panoramic view of City Square reveals it to be the result of two separate photographs. The big giveaway is the fact that the van in the bottom left with the word "Selecta" on its side also appears in front of the Post Office. The crater in the foreground was where the Royal Exchange building had stood. An office block was built on the site soon after. The Majestic cinema stands directly opposite, built in 1921 before the art-deco style had taken hold with cinema designers. Even thought this picture is less than thirty-five years old, it is remarkable that every single car, van and lorry pictured in this busy scene was British made. Just as if to confirm its place as a high class city hotel, the Queen's has no less than two Jaguar saloons parked outside its foyer.

From Founder to Grandson
70 years of tradition maintained.

Robert Barr, founder of the Barr and Wallace Arnold Trust

Wallace Arnold Tours carries thousands of people each year to destinations throughout Britain and Europe. Its coach fleet is Britain's most modern.

But its roots can be traced back as far as 1912 when Robert Barr bought his first vehicle, a Karrier which operated as a lorry in Leeds during the week and as a charabanc for country trips at weekends.

Early expansion.

The springboard for expansion really began in 1926 when he took over the partnership of Wallace Cunningham and Arnold Crowe, Leeds charabanc operators who traded as Wallace Arnold.

Much has happened since then. By 1930 the coach fleet numbered 15 vehicles and by the end of the decade had doubled to 30.

In 1939-40 the government requisitioned a dozen coaches for use as ambulances and troop carriers to aid the war effort. In the summer of 46 new Wallace Arnold coaches were on the road. With those who could afford new cars having to join a two year waiting list, coach travel reached new heights of popularity.

Early post war publicity aimed at the American market offered four tours from London. In addition a 'delightful' selection of motor coach tours from Yorkshire was offered to American clientele with rail travel from London to Leeds and overnight accommodation in Leeds before and after the tour. The company even produced brochures for North America with dollar prices. A 14 day tour of the Scottish Highlands which actually got no further than Aberdeen, cost $190 in 1949.

Without doubt, the 1950s were the golden days of coach excursions. At the height of the boom period, Wallace Arnold was offering eight continental tours to Switzerland, France, Austria, Italy, Holland and Spain with - wait for it - prices ranging from 35-37 guineas (£36.75 to £38.85).

Two of the tours offered only one departure each year, but others operated up to nine times in any one season. Day tours with Wallace Arnold from Scarborough, ranged from 1s 3d (6p) for a short circular tour of the immediate area to 13s (65p) for a day at Stokesley and the Cleveland Hills.

Opening up a market

Robert Barr's expansion plans continued to flourish with the purchase of various other carriers in Leeds and Scarborough. By the mid 50s Wallace Arnold

Above: The first bus in the fleet, in 1919, was this 28 seat solid tyred Karrier. This substantial looking bus weighed only four tons unladen.

claimed to be carrying over 25,000 tour passengers every year. The company also became one of the

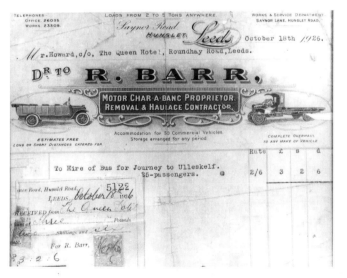

first British coach operators to provide low-priced off season holidays, thereby opening up a market which was to grow dramatically.

In 1961 Wallace Arnold announced a record number of coach holiday bookings. The continental holiday programme now included not only coach tours - which now embraced Norway - but also holidays by air, sea and rail.

The 70s saw a steady decline in day trips as increased car ownership began to bite. On the other hand continental holidays began to expand rapidly. In 1971 Wallace Arnold's continental tour programme offered 38,000 seats. This was increased to 42,000 by 1972 - a rise of 10%.

Agreement was reached in 1975 with operators in Paris and Florence for a

jointly operated express service, linking London, Paris, Lyon, Turin, Genoa, Florence and Rome. Following European red tape, the launch of this cross European service got under way in 1977, running once a week in summer. The end to end journey time was 37 hours with a return fare of £63.

Above: A 1926 invoice for a trip to Ulleskelf, costing £3 2s 6d. Storage, removals and overhauls were amongst the other services offered. Top: There was a pent-up demand in Britain when the war ended as this queue outside the Corn Exchange in 1945 graphically illustrates. They were waiting to book Wallace Arnold coastal express services. Right: Staff outings were a major highlight of the year. Such an example is this one in 1923 from Schofields in Leeds.

Memories of Leeds

Left: *Outings to the coast by Working Mens Clubs were a popular feature of the early 1950s as shown by this splendid line of Wallace Arnold coaches ready for departure. The exact location and occasion of this wonderful picture are lost in the mists of time.*

Right: *Robert Barr, standing on the far right, poses with a number of happy passengers about to board the Leeds Mercury escorted motor tour in 1937. The Leyland Tiger coach pictured was requisitioned by the Air Force in 1939.*

Below: *Wallace Arnold's Leeds booking office in 1953. Note the coronation poster above the counter clerk.*

Below right: *During the 1950s the Company owned two bus companies in Leeds - Kippax and District and Farsley Omnibus. A bus belonging to the latter Company is seen at Stanningley Bottom showing a family complete with collapsible push chair.*

Moscow targeted

With the success of this service, Wallace Arnold set its sights on a prize destination - MOSCOW - then still firmly behind the iron curtain. During 1977 negotiations were concluded for a joint service to start in 1979.

Meanwhile, the Dream Holidays for the Elderly was becoming increasingly important and by 1979 had been rebranded as Supersaver Holidays for the Older Holidaymaker. The decade closed with Wallace Arnold carrying 2.5 million people and covering many millions of miles a year.

Cruise holidays became a focus of attention for the company in 1980. In linking up with P&O Cruises, Wallace Arnold launched a series of European holidays which combined coach travel with cruising on the P&O's Canberra and Oriana liners. Prices started at £364 for 12 days using the coach between Britain and Nice and returning by sea - or vice versa.

Left: The Kippax and District Motor Company was bought by Wallace Arnold in 1956 - one of its buses is shown crossing City Square. Below: The Calls Coach Station behind the Corn Exchange was the centre of the Company's operation in Leeds. Two photographs taken in 1958 and 1964 show coaches loading prior to departure on tour.

It was a time of change in the structure of the coach market and a new strategy was devised by the company to cope with this. Its aim was summed up in the 1987 annual report:

"Our strategy is to offer good quality, value for money services; operate the most modern fleet of coaches in the country and to provide a highly efficient booking service".

The reservation system had been fully computerised since 1982 but from 1985 a new on-line system gave travel agents direct access. The system was further updated at a cost of almost £1,000,000 in 1989. This was an especially good period for the company as continuing improvements in its performance earned it the accolade of "Top Coach Operator" in 1988 and 1989. Accolades which have been repeated at various intervals ever since, culminating in the most recent award of "Best British and European Tour Programme 1995/96".

Despite the economic recession which gripped the county at the start of the 90s, Wallace Arnold retained its extensive and innovative programme, its investment in new coaches and its profitability.

Some areas provided growth opportunities like Southern Ireland through a combination of coach/sea and coach/air holidays.

On the continental front the majority of holidays were and are now run by the company's own vehicles although this did not prevent new links with France's prestigious high speed train (the TGV) to whisk holiday makers south from Paris after being taken there by coach from Britain.

And with the opening of the Channel Tunnel, new holidays were promoted using the EuroStar train service.

For those travellers who liked to spend time at sea,

the company used a new ferry/cruise service run by P&O from Portsmouth to Bilbao as an alternative to travelling by coach through France to get to Spain.

Guaranteed Quality

Nearer to home, Wallace Arnold was investing in hotels to ensure it could offer guaranteed quality standards. The Grand in Exmouth, the Broadway Park at Sandown on the Isle of Wight, the Burlington at Eastbourne, the Savoy at Bournemouth and the Trecarn at Babbacombe are today a true measure of the highest quality in food, accommodation and entertainment.

Indeed a far cry from Robert Barr's pioneering trips with a solid-tyred charabanc, but progress of which he would have been justly proud.

And there is still a Robert Barr with the company - grandson of the founder and Chairman of the Leisure division - so maintaining the family tradition of the company and the quality standards in which it places such store.

The pioneering spirit in providing the utmost in customer care is also very much to the fore through the continuous introduction of new benefits the latest of which - a Total Luggage Handling Service - exemplifies the company's commitment to the very best in customer service.

Above: Wallace Arnold as befits Yorkshire's major coach operator has played a key part in significant sporting events in the area. This is the return of the Leeds United team from the cup final in 1965. How many players of the Revie era do you recognise?

Lewis's was for many years considered the "Harrods of the North". Construction began on the building in the early 1930s, when the site cost £160,000 to acquire and the building itself another £750,000. Initially of just three storeys, more floors were added in later years. Lewis's great rival, Schofield's was opened by Snowden Schofield in 1902 and the first day's takings amounted to £62 3s. This 1949 picture of post war Leeds makes an interesting contrast with the earlier wartime picture from the same vantage point (see *Wartime Leeds*). Rationing and a general lack of prosperity in the immediate post war years meant that retailers like Lewis's had hard times until the economy picked up as the 1950s progressed.

Generations of shoppers from Leeds and much further afield have regarded a shopping trip to the city centre as somewhat of a treat, an occasion reserved for buying that special item. And what better place to start than Bond Street, pictured here in the late 1940s. Today, this area is part of the pedestrianised core of the city centre shopping area and was heavily redeveloped in the 1960s, making it unrecognisable from the scene captured above. Yellow lines would not appear on Leeds' streets for another fifteen years after this picture, allowing easy access for customers of such high quality establishments as Jaeger House. The Yorkshire Post had their offices in Bond Street, visible towards the right of this photograph.

The different styles of the ornate building facades on Briggate can be clearly seen in this 1946 photograph, which conspire with the extensive advertising signs to create a slightly chaotic image. The planning laws relating to shop signs appear to have been much more relaxed than they are today, allowing a less sanitised appearance to streets like Briggate. The Police box in the foreground harks back to days when the bobby on the beat relied on a whistle to keep in touch with base whilst walking his patch, rather than the walkie-talkie that became the norm in the mid 1960s.

Briggate again, this time in 1937. The Kardomah Café was a favoured refreshment venue for many thirsty shoppers, eager to sample their tea and cakes in the days before fast food outlets were the norm on British high streets. The Bon Marché shop has its blinds pulled down, shielding the contents of its shop window from the sun. Virtually every shop had blinds and they were oft as not pulled down, making the pavement a haven from sun or rain. Little things like this are what really bring back childhood memories of shopping, hand in hand with mum, for many folk. The Great Universal Stores, pictured further along Briggate, were later to become pioneers of mail-order shopping.

Left: The Queens Arcade, opened in 1899 on the site of the Rose and Crown Yard, is pictured here in the late 1960s. The first arcade to be opened in the city was Thornton's Arcade, built in 1878. The design of many of these ornate Victorian structures was driven by the need to fit as many shops into as confined an area as possible.

Right: The County Arcade, shown here in the late 1960s, was built in 1903 and contained 45 shops when it first opened, as well as a cafe restaurant. Its fine architecture still serves to impress today, complete with its marble pillars and mosaic floor. The Yorkshire Post carried an article in 1903 describing the County as "The prettiest shopping avenue in the city."

The 1930s were a great time for the cinema industry, with the growth in the popularity of "talkies", resulting in an ambitious cinema building programme across the country. These three examples were constructed in that decade and they all exhibit elements of the art-deco style so beloved by 1930s architects.

Right: The Kingsway on Harrogate Road is pictured shortly after its opening in June 1937. Designed by James Brodie of Pudsey, this great picture house showed its last film in the late 1950s, before becoming a synagogue.

Below right: People driving through Harehills today cannot fail to spot the building that was formerly the Clock Cinema, even though it now serves as a hi-fi showroom. In its days as a cinema it boasted such 1930s luxury fittings as a fountain in its foyer.

Below: The Dominion Cinema on Harrogate Road in the late 1930s. The cyclist casually stood by the gas lamp would be less likely to hang around the same spot today, such is the volume of traffic on this part of Harrogate Road.

The City Varieties, second home to some of the world's theatrical greats...

The day that British troops relieved the Garrison at Mafeking after a seventeen month siege by the Boers was one of unrestrained jubilation in a tiny music hall in Leeds by the name of City Varieties, where comedian Charles Coburn was halfway through a week at the top of the bill.

Among his audience were British soldiers about to join their comrades in South Africa, as well as the families of men who were already out there fighting.

Coburn was to carry on to become one of the 'greats' of British music hall entertainment - so many of whom owe their careers to the City Varieties, where a good reception virtually stamped the seal of success to up and coming performers.

Big Names
Bud Flanagan, Lily Langtry, Houdini, Dan Leno, Fred Karno and the legendary Marie Lloyd all played at City Varieties. A house of entertainment has existed between the Headrow and Briggate for over 200 years, although at first it was just a 'singing room' attached to the White Swan public house.

The Fashionable Lounge
It has gradually developed its identity as a variety music hall, with one of its greatest boosts being the opening of Thornton's Fashionable Lounge in 1865. At that time people were still being publicly hanged and for most of Britain's people, life was endured, not lived. So when they could afford the admission price of only pennies, the people would flock to the Fashionable Lounge to see up to a dozen acts in an atmosphere heavy with cigar smoke and plenty of ale to liven the spirits.

For many, a night of Vaudeville was their only bright spot in a hard week's toil in the woollen mills of industrial West Yorkshire.

Cradle of Talent

The greatest entertainer whose early days included performances at the City Varieties was a youngster who in 1896 joined an act known as Eight Lancashire Lads. A year later, he came to Leeds to do a week at the Varieties. clog dancing and doing the 'cake-walk'. Eighteen years of Vaudeville followed until he made his first film, The Little Tramp - otherwise known as Charlie Chaplin.

The Good Old Days

In the main, the City Varieties is best known for its popular entertainment and in particular for "The Good Old Days" series (the longest running television programme in the world) which were filmed from the theatre.

Above: This photograph, dating from c 1900 shows that the City Varieties has always been as popular as it is today.

Facing page and below left: Both of these photographs were captured during the filming of the Good Old Days - the world's longest running television programme.

Right: Charlie Chaplin, later to become one of Hollywood's pioneers, spent some of his early days treading the boards at the City Varieties in a troupe called "Eight Lancashire Lads".

The contrast between the new buildings and older ones is clear in this 1938 aerial view, with the longer established premises characterised by their blackened exteriors. Many of the city's more prominent buildings can be seen either in the process of being constructed or have just been completed. The Civic centre is one example of the latter, its clean Portland stone facade visible on the bottom left. Over 90 per cent of the workers employed to build the Civic Centre were taken from the city's unemployment register. Other construction projects visible include Lewis's, Quarry Hill Flats and the Brotherton Wing of the Leeds General Infirmary.

The long shadows show this to be a morning picture, taken in late 1936 as the building work on the new Queen's Hotel progressed towards completion. The number of cars, trams and people visible around City Square and Park Row suggest a this was a weekday. The hotel would be opened by the Earl of Harewood the year after this photograph was taken. The railway and its various sidings can be seen, alongside the River Aire in this view as a man-made division between the shops and commercial properties and the city centre and what lay beyond, the mainly industrial land to the south of the station.

Leeds saw a great deal of redevelopment in the 1960s, in common with just about every other city in the country as the economic boom of that decade took off. Some of the city's more controversial buildings were created in the 60s, amongst them the Merrion Centre.

Following the pattern of the time, the Merrion Centre was designed with square modernist lines cast in concrete. The site of the shopping centre was, at the turn of the century, known as The Leylands, an area mainly populated by poor jewish immigrants, drawn to Leeds by the availability of work in the clothing industry.

Another 1960s invention is visible in this view, the multi-storey car park. The need for these was brought on by the increasing popularity of the motor car, which had seen tremendous growth in the post war period. The Locarno ballroom formed part of the Merrion Centre when this picture was taken, later to become Rockefella's, with a certain Jimmy Savile as the resident Disc Jockey.

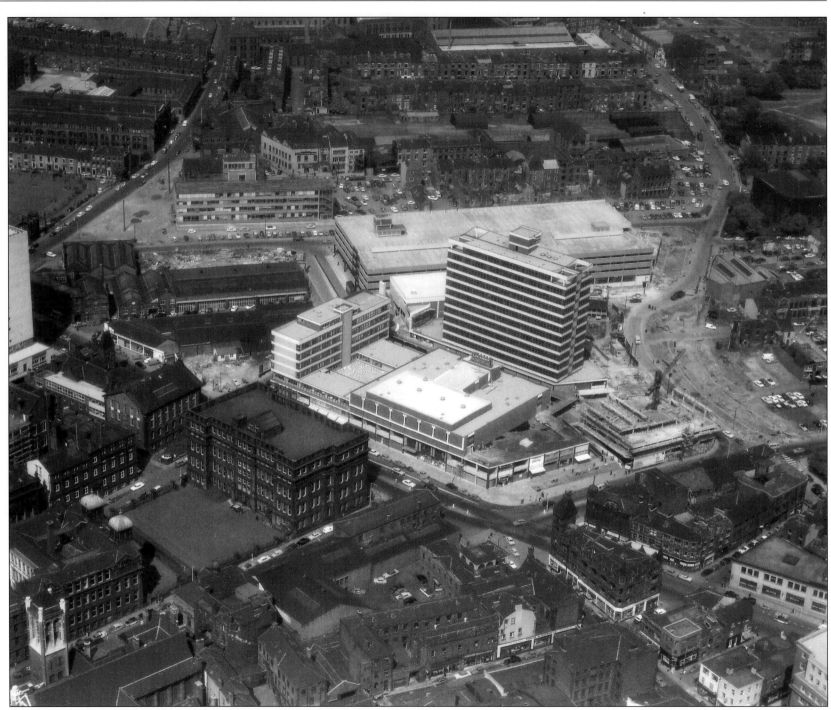

Probably the civil engineering project to have most impact on day-to-day Leeds life, the construction of the Inner Ring Road is shown here in 1966, looking at Clay Pit Lane. Traffic levels rose sharply in the 1960s and the need for a road to bypass the city centre of Leeds became apparent. The policy of separating vehicle traffic from pedestrians in city centres gathered momentum as the decade progressed.

The course of the inner Ring Road had quite a long way to run, as this view shows, with the Quarry Hill Flats, seen at the top of the photograph, providing a good reference point for the eventual path that the road would follow.

The physical landscape of the city changed during the 1960s more than in any other decade before or since, with the scale of redevelopment driven by the economic boom that the city enjoyed. Coupled with the explosion of popular culture that characterised the 1960s, it is no surprise that it this period of our recent history is often dubbed the "decade of change".

This late 1950s aerial view of Leeds city centre looking east to west provides a glimpse of how things looked in post war Leeds before the wholesale changes that were to follow in the 1960s. The long curve of Quarry Hill Flats in the foreground gives way to the bus station and markets area, which remains relatively unchanged to this day. Bearing in mind the number of towns and cities that have seen their Victorian market halls demolished to make way for inferior concrete replacements, this is a great blessing. Even forty years ago, parking was at a premium in the city.

Its position alongside the Inner Ring Road, complete with electronic neon clock, makes the Yorkshire Post Building one of the city's more prominent landmarks. Opened in 1970 by the Prince of Wales, its design does give away its 1960s conception. The Inner Ring Road would make an impact on the area in front of the Yorkshire Post building soon after this picture was taken. A few hundred yards away, the Leeds International Swimming Pool was also in the process of being built.

Leeds Civic Theatre

Cookridge Street, Leeds LS2 8BH
Tel: 0113 245 6343 Fax: 0113 234 7973

The box office is open Monday to Saturday
from **10am** to **8pm**
Telephone *0113 245 5505* or *0113 247 6962*
For further information telephone
the General Manager, Steven Cartwright
on **0113 245 6343**

Leeds Civic Theatre: Giving Everyone the chance to 'Tread the Boards'

The Leeds Civic Theatre has been subject to many changes since the 1920s. Designed as, to give it its full title, 'The Leeds Institute of Arts and Sciences', by Cuthbert Broderick in 1868, it was originally a lecture hall. With dwindling membership of the Institute, the main lecture hall was used more and more as a venue for theatrical performers. In 1939 the Institute came to an end and the building was purchased by the City of Leeds.

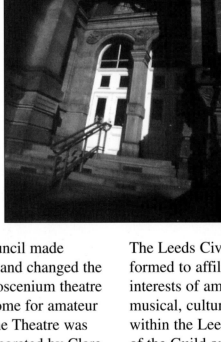

After the war the council made extensive alterations and changed the lecture hall into a proscenium theatre which became the home for amateur theatre.   In 1983, the Theatre was refurbished and redecorated by Clare Ferraby who, the year before, had undertaken the magnificent restoration of the Leeds Grand Theatre. The seating was rearranged and the proscenium wall completely reconstructed. The auditorium was redecorated and the magnificent gasolier was restored and illuminated with profile (spot) lights. The ceiling decoration included star stencilling and some of these stars are gilded with pure gold leaf. The colours are taken from the beautiful, original tiles which are around the back of the side stalls.

The Leeds Civic Arts Guild was formed to affiliate the common interests of amateur dramatic, musical, cultural and artistic societies within the Leeds area. The objectives of the Guild are to co-ordinate the activities of the affiliated societies, particularly in relation to the use of the Civic Theatre, the rehearsal rooms and other such facilities as may, from time to time, be provided for them by Leeds City Council. The Guild is privileged to have as its home the Civic Theatre which is one of the finest facilities in the country given over to the use of amateur societies. Many societies continue to use the facilities to the full and a wide and varied programme is presented for around 45 weeks of the year. The policy of presenting professional productions on the remaining available dates not only serves to maximise the use of the theatre, but also helps to attract new audiences who might, hopefully, become regular visitors. The Guild's amateur productions are carefully adjudicated by the Guild Executive Committee. All aspects of

the productions are judged and a high standard is expected. This is further encouraged by the Guild's 'Presentation Evening' held once a year, where trophies for Best Production, Best Actor and Best Set are awarded during an evening often attended by a Civic Dignitary, so a lot of good natured competition to win one of these coveted trophies ensures a very professional attitude towards the productions. New patrons are often surprised to find that the Civic, far from being an 'amateur' venue, provides excellent entertainment in a 'proper' theatre at prices a fraction of the cost of others in the area. The theatre has had its share of famous actors and TV presenters who first 'trod the boards' at the Civic.

These include Peter O'Toole, Ron Pickup, Bob Peck and at least four of the cast of Coronation Street in recent years. Scriptwriter, Barry Cryer and TV presenter Mark Curry are also listed amongst the Guild Hall of

Fame. Highly talented or just enthusiastic new members are always welcome to join one of the many different societies. In addition to the entertainments policy, the Civic Theatre is also available for conferences, seminars, meetings, functions etc. In recent years a one day UFO conference gathered such popularity it was extended to three days. Leeds Civic Theatre's ever popular Pantomime is rapidly becoming a traditional family outing running from the beginning of December and continuing throughout the whole of the Christmas holiday and into the New Year.

Delighting audiences for more than a century

Leeds Grand Theatre has captivated audiences with a wealth of entertainment ranging from ballet, review and comedy to drama, opera, musicals and pantomime for more than a century.

Leeds Grand Theatre is synonymous with all that is best in the performing arts. For the past 18 years it has been home to Opera North, one of the best-loved and most respected opera companies in Britain. It frequently stages hit West End and Broadway musicals and continues to attract the biggest names in show business to perform on its stage.

Over the years the theatre has established and maintained close associations with some of the most prestigious touring companies including Northern Ballet Theatre and English National Ballet in addition to local amateur operatic and dramatic societies.

Since its opening on 18th November 1878 all the great names of theatre have trodden the boards at Leeds Grand-Ellen Terry, Lily Langtry, Sarah Bernhardt, Sir Laurence Olivier, Dame Sybil Thorndike and Ivor Novello.

In more recent years the theatre has witnessed performances by Deborah Kerr, Ken Dodd, Tommy Steele, David Essex, Ben Elton, Hank Martin and a galaxy of other stars.

With a seating capacity of 1,550, The Grand is the largest theatre in Leeds. It has a classic Victorian proscenium stage with stalls, dress circle, upper circle, balconies and boxes. Built by architect George Corson, the theatre is a mixture of styles with a Gothic facade that belies the interior splendour.

Today Leeds Grand Theatre is recognised as a centre of excellence for entertainment and culture in the North of England and as one of the most successful theatres in the country.

The Grand Theatre and Opera House

46 New Briggate, Leeds LS 1 1NZ

Box Office : (0113) 245 9351

(0113) 244 0971

(open 10am to 9.00pm Mon - Sat & 11.30am to 7.00pm Sun)

Tel: (0113) 245 6014   Fax: (0113) 246 5906

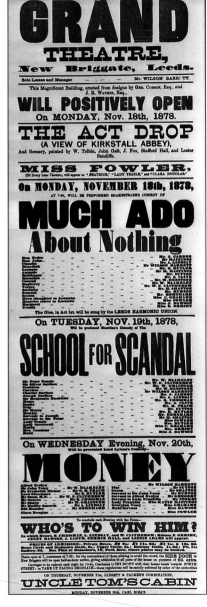

Advertising poster dating from 1878

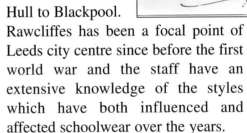
Memories of Leeds

Rawcliffes: A century of school wear in Leeds.

The North of England's largest school outfitter celebrates its centennial year in 1997 and throughout its 100 years trading has enjoyed prime locations on town centre high streets in cities from Leeds to Stockton, Hull to Blackpool.

Rawcliffes has been a focal point of Leeds city centre since before the first world war and the staff have an extensive knowledge of the styles which have both influenced and affected schoolwear over the years.

A family business, Rawcliffes has successfully traded from their location on Duncan Street for over 80 years, and the company still places great emphasis on maintaining its policy of providing value for money, excellent service and unbeatable quality.

Over the years Rawcliffes has provided uniforms for generations of school children and now utilise a vast experience and knowledge of the school wear industry to move with the times, continually updating current

schoolwear trends to keep Rawcliffes as popular today as it was when it first began almost a century ago.

Rawcliffes has seen many new styles evolve in this time and although the changes have not always been drastic ones and the traditional school uniform certainly still has its place, there can be no doubt that the modern, versatile trends of today appeal to both pupils and parents, as well as to the schools themselves.

In recent years Rawcliffes has also expanded to sell a comprehensive selection of top brand sportswear and equipment including Nike, Reebok, Adidas, Ellesse and Mizuno, making the company a one-stop-shop for all school and sportswear needs.

These days, children are increasingly image conscious and Rawcliffes are a company who pride themselves on keeping up to date with current trends. It is no wonder then, that Rawcliffes' extensive range of school and

OUR PROMISE

ASDA was founded on the principles of good, honest value and, right from the start, we made a promise to all our customers to offer them permanently low prices on all their weekly shopping. Today at ASDA, we are still making the same promise that we made all those years ago and we still offer the finest quality at the lowest possible prices. We still believe in our founding principles, and that a promise should be forever.

ASDA

POCKET THE DIFFERENCE

www.asda.co.uk

ASDA: From Small Beginnings To Big News

ASDA is famous for its quality produce and permanently low prices, stocking everything from George clothing to freshly baked bread. ASDA have always focused on giving customers the best possible service and the best value products. It may therefore come as a surprise then to learn that its roots are embedded in the dairy business, going as far back as the 1920s.

However, it was not until 1949, that Associated Dairies was formed. This was to become the backbone of the ASDA, that shoppers know and love. It was through Associated Dairies that Peter and Fred Asquith were able to purchase their first property in Pontefract and by the mid 1950s they were able to obtain planning permission to build a supermarket. This broke away from the traditional mould of shopkeeping.

It was the brothers hard work and imagination that turned this property into a thriving business. The Queens Theatre in Castleford needed a new floor - they laid it themselves. They stocked all the shelves and cut their prices. The result - lots of satisfied customers.

The brothers worked with Sir Noel Stockdale to take ASDA one step further. They bought a store at South

In December 1966 supermarkets were still quite a novelty. This scene is of the newly opened Queen's Supermarket, later to become ASDA, at Crossgates.

Elmsall near Wakefield which had an enormous car park. Thus the era of park and shop was born. ASDA established their retailing principles; unbeatable, branded products with labels that you recognised at prices that customers could not believe.

Not satisfied with this, attention was turned to Nottingham and the purchase of a store 20 times bigger than South Elmsall. ASDA's retailing principles may have been fixed, but the mix of products on sale was not. If customers shopped at

ASDA, they could get everything they needed under one roof. By 1970, only a third of the floor space was taken up with food, the rest was filled with a variety of household goods.

It was at this time that ASDA headed south. The opening of the South Woodham Ferrers store in 1977 heralded a new way of working. Not only did the store have to be efficient at supplying the cut price products, but it had to look good as well.

During the 1980s, the company underwent enormous change and development. ASDA colleagues went through rigorous training to ensure that customer service was second to none. This has developed to the extent that ASDA now offer a bag packing service, carry to car service, big shopper checkouts, brolley patrols and pet stops.

This drive for continual improvement has been reflected in the development of the Tell Archie suggestion scheme, where colleagues are encouraged to send in suggestions to help cut costs and improve the business. It is by encouraging this change, that ASDA can continue to offer permanently low prices to all of their customers - and that's forever!

Redmayne-Bentley,

In December 1875 John Redmayne laid down his pen and climbed off his high stool for the last time at the offices of the Yorkshire Banking Company (later to become part of Midland Bank) in City Square Leeds. He had taken the bold step to set up

as a Stockbroker on his own account. The Stock Exchange had come to Leeds in the 1845/46 Great Rail Boom. In the 1870s Leeds was still regarded as an important centre in the trading in railway shares. John

Redmayne was later to visit the USA and be introduced to brokers in New York and Boston, Mass, as an expert on "rails".

Redmayne's main business has always been the provision of a first class service to private clients, either directly or via intermediaries, eg solicitors, accountants or bank branches.

A great step forward was made when

Stockbrokers in Leeds since 1876

Gavin Loudon, father of the present Senior Partner Keith Loudon, organised the merger of Redmayne & Co and F W Bentley & Co, taking over the business of J W Granger & Co.

The "Big Bang" in 1986 changed the mould of the Stock Exchange. The conventional wisdom of the time was that firms had to be part of large conglomerates and specialise in either "discounting", giving a no frills, no advice service at low cost, or specialise in giving a portfolio service to "big net worth" clients. Redmayne-Bentley took a counter view. They determined to remain a three-partner firm and to charge a competitive commission scale though not the cheapest. The firm prospered.

In the following years teams of stockbrokers in various parts of the country liked the Redmayne-Bentley "style" and approached the firm to develop a closer association. The result of this is that Redmayne-

Bentley now have 15 branches from Inverness and Perth in the North to Henley-on-Thames and Leigh-on-Sea in the South.

Over the years the firm has always been a leader and innovator. For example, they were the first firm in Leeds to install a teleprinter - many, many years ago. In more recent times Redmayne-Bentley were amongst the first to introduce client cards - "Sharecards" - and try television advertising. 1995 saw Redmayne-Bentley take space on the "Internet".

Redmayne-Bentley's status was recognised in 1995 when they were voted runners up in an Investors Chronicle readers poll in the category Dealing with Advice. In 1996 there was great delight when Redmayne-

Bentley were voted joint winners.

Communication with clients has always been a top priority for Redmayne-Bentley. Regular Newsletters, seminar programmes, etc. have been on the agenda for a number of years.

Redmayne-Bentley are delighted to be involved with the Investors Breakfast with Jim Slater on the subject of Extraordinary Profits from Growth Shares. The policy of the company is aiming to give their clients the best possible service and to help them with advice and information.

Above left: This photograph dates from 1962 and highlights the change from todays hi-tech world of stockbroking where computers play a large part.

Facing page: A contract note dating from 1961, a time when most records were still manually produced in fountain pen script.

A. Taylor & Son (Leeds) Ltd - Fabrication & Machining Engineers

The company was originally founded in 1864 by Albert Taylor, a tinsmith and sheetmetal worker in premises just off Kirkstall Road, about half a mile away from the present site.

During the war years their main product was bomb tail fins and then in 1947 TW Jeffery bought the company from the grandson of the original founder and the business developed into sheetmetal and light fabrications for mechanical handling schemes, elevators, conveyors, hoppers etc.

Early in 1948 HW Benson (Bill), the present chairman, joined the company as assistant works manager and expansion continued including what was to become a large department manufacturing ductwork for air treatment systems, these being installed on sites all over the UK.

During the 1950s the fabrication side became involved in the manufacture of steeping cisterns, grist cases, etc., for the Scottish whisky distilleries. These were installed by the erection teams

employed by the company.

This led to the fabrication of much larger and heavier products which could only be done by moving into larger premises and heavier machinery.

By this time Bill Benson had been appointed to the board with a minor shareholding, and in 1975 negotiations began with TW Jeffery to take over the shareholding as he wished to retire.

This was achieved in 1976, giving the Benson family complete control and allowing Bill and his son John, the present managing director to develop the company further.

The premises were purchased, more overhead cranes and much heavier machinery were installed. With the highly skilled labour force and plant available, Taylor's was to obtain contracts for the fabrication and machining of guide bases, drill templates, christmas tree structures etc., to be used on the North Sea oil and gas wells.

1985 saw the appointment of Russell Greenwood to the position of Assistant Works Manager, having brought with him a wealth of welding experience

and expertise which was second to none. He quickly rose to his present position of Works Director.

The purchase of adjoining premises has allowed further expansion, with a natural progression into NDT, proof load testing and a machine tool facility devoted to horizontal and vertical boring, turning and milling etc.

A dedicated staff and workforce should enable the company to move smoothly into the 21st century.

Above: Dust cover for an inclined coke screen.

Left: An insulated road tanker.

From Switzerland to Horsforth...

The story of two great scientists who created a successful Leeds based chemical company.

The history of Sandoz (the Speciality Chemicals part of which is now renamed Clariant) is directly linked to an event that revolutionised the way we see the world.

In 1856 a British chemist Sir William Henry Perkin was attempting to synthesise the anti-malaria drug quinine from coal tar. During his experiments he accidentally produced a soluble purple dye, which eventually became the world's first synthetic dye that was practical to produce on a commercial basis. The colour revolution had begun.

By 1886 the potential of Perkin's discovery had become clear to two innovative Swiss entrepreneurs, chemist Dr Alfred Kern and his partner Edouard Sandoz. They founded the Kern and Sandoz Company in Basle, Switzerland and

began production of the new coal tar, or aniline dyes at the rate of some twelve tons per year.

From modest beginnings the company gradually grew and prospered, and in 1911 the

partners decided to expand. Appropriately enough, the first Sandoz company outside Switzerland was established in the heart of the English wool textile industry in Canal Road in Bradford, where it remained for approximately the next 50 years. Then as the company developed further a move was made to a 48 acre greenfield site in Horsforth near Leeds.

This site, partly hidden in the valley, is close to the

ring road and has been the base since 1961 of both the chemicals and pharmaceuticals divisions of Sandoz. The 1990s heralded many changes and on 1st July 1995 the Chemicals Division of Sandoz separated from the rest of the group and became an independent company known as Clariant. By the middle of 1997, the name of Sandoz will have disappeared completely from Horsforth following the merger of Sandoz Pharmaceuticals with Ciba to form a new company - Novartis.

With headquarters in Muttenz, Switzerland and around 8400 employees worldwide, Clariant is a leading company in the research, development, production and marketing of dyes and chemicals. It serves a wide range of industries and its dyes, pigments and speciality chemicals can be found in many products that people use every day.

There are now around 420 people employed by Clariant UK on the Horsforth site which houses Administration, Production, Distribution and Research & Development facilities as well as being the international headquarters for Clariant sales to the paper industry throughout the world.

Clariant strive to achieve total quality in everything they do, from the products they make to the customer service they provide. As a result of their efforts, they were one of the first companies in Britain to achieve certification to the BS 5750 Part I Quality Assurance standard now the BS EN ISO 9001:1994 International Standard. Their ISO 9001 Quality System is the foundation for their drive for quality and their Continuous Improvement Programme. This is an ongoing, quality enhancing initiative aimed at improving all their business activities from Customer Service, Production and Supply through to Safety, Health and Environmental Protection.

In 1990 some £12 million was spent on the development of a sophisticated automated high bay warehouse, with its associated fire and waste water holding tanks, and effluent pre-treatment facilities. This together with installation of a modern automated tank farm has dramatically increased storage and distribution efficiency, whilst making significant contribution to the company's safety and environmental commitment.

As a member of the Chemical Industries Association, Clariant UK Ltd is also actively involved with the industry's Responsible Care programme.

These and many other initiatives are enabling Clariant to work more closely than ever with major customer groups to solve problems and create the advanced new products demanded by today's sophisticated consumers.

Above: The Horsforth site of Clariant UK Ltd, formerly known as Sandoz, taken in about 1962.
Facing page, top left: Edouard Sandoz.
Facing page, bottom left: Doctor Alfred Kern.
Facing page, top right: Laboratory workers in the 1940s; many industries relied on female labour during the war years.
Facing Page, bottom right: The Canal Road site in Bradford.
Left : A wartime picture depicting the Canal Road site before it was constructed.

A modern business that began with one man and an idea in 1885...

Frank Horsell

Horsell's association with the printing industry can be traced back over a century. In 1885 Frank Horsell, with two assistants, rented a small but respectable factory in Meadow Lane, Leeds and started a business in covering and renovating the inking rollers used by litho printers. Forward thinking, Frank Horsell bought a weaving mill at this time to manufacture the sleeves.

Within two years Frank Horsell had increased his workforce to ten and it became clear that larger premises were needed. Manufacture and supply of the ink roller sleeves led logically to the supply of inks themselves and a colour grinding business was started in 1894 which was moved six years later to premises in Victoria Road, Leeds.

In the early days of printing, most printers concocted their own inks from ingredients such as lamp-black and molasses.

In 1906 Frank Horsell expanded his business to include the manufacture of printing plates. In this way the company ventured into a new market where it would eventually achieve it's biggest growth.

In 1985 Horsell was sold to Cookson PLC; transforming a family run business into a major company within the international arena. The significant investment resulted in the acquisition of both Freundorfer GmbH in Munich, Germany and Anchor Inc. in Jacksonville, US. Then in 1990, the Horsell group of companies was bought by International Paper Inc., the largest paper company in the world, to become part of its Imaging Products Division.

Albion Street, Leeds in 1910. Henry Inchbold, who owned the shop on the right was Chairman of Horsells in 1890.

As well as Horsell, Imaging Products Division is comprised of three other major print and pre-press manufacturers. Anitec the film manufacturer based in New York, Ilford the specialists in black and white photography and Anchor the major name in pressroom chemicals. As a company Horsell Anitec now offers the full range of consumables and equipment from Electronic Imaging through to press room.

Technology within the printing industry is developing and advancing rapidly. As a major player within the printing industry, Horsell Anitec ensures that it is at the forefront of technological advancement and is well positioned to offer products with real competitive advantage. The Research and Development team is currently developing Computer-to-Plate technologies, which will enable customers to produce press ready printing plates quicker, more cost effective and environmentally friendly than ever before. Horsell Anitec's continual commitment to improving products and services shall ensure the future success of this Leeds based company.

Far Left: An illustration from Horsell's 1911 price list, showing their litho roller covering machine, sold at £20 complete.

Horsell Anitec

Head Office: Nepshaw Lane South, Gildersome, Morley, Leeds LS27 0QT
Tel 0113 252 2177   Fax 0113 252 7501

Wm Dodgson & Son: Serving Leeds for over 150 Years

William Dodgson & Son was founded in 1842 by William Dodgson, a joiner and undertaker who worked from a joiners shop in Shannon Street. He was succeeded by John Dodgson who in addition to joinery and undertaking also built rows of back-to-back houses in partnership with local builders. The streets in which the houses were built were named after his relatives, indeed Ada Crescent and Bertha Street were named after his daughters. Before long the success of the business led to the need for new premises and the company moved to Beckett Street.

After John's death in 1938 his sons, Lindley and William, succeeded him. They moved the business again, to Cowper Grove, into purpose built premises which included a chapel of rest (a pioneering concept in Leeds at the time). Prior to this the deceased remained at home until the time of the funeral.

They were then joined by William's son, who was also called William, and bought their first motorised fleet including a Rolls-Royce hearse. This was possible due to the continued success of the company, gained by the quality of personal service and traditional values and courtesies. At the same time the joinery side of the business was adapted to specialise in the construction of coffins. Lindley Dodgson (see picture, right) died in

Left: This photograph was taken after William Dodgson, the senior partner in the firm had been installed as National President of the NAFD in 1968. He is pictured in the centre, with his son Martin on his right and his father, William on his left.
Right: The first Rolls-Royce hearse, dating from the 1930s.
Above, right: Mr Lindley Dodgson.

1953 but three years later the fifth generation of Dodgson's joined the company. Martin Dodgson was 16 when he first began working for the firm and was the first member of the family to be sent on a two and a half year course in London to study undertaking.

The business expanded and soon outgrew the Cowper Grove premises and moved to its present site in 1970 where today, it still serves the Leeds area. The property has a number of chapels of rest and on the same site, a catering facility.

William Dodgson lived long enough to see the redevelopments but sadly died, in 1971. During his life he served as National President of the National Association of Funeral Directors, a position taken up by his son some years later. The business continued to prosper under he expert guidance of William and Martin. Martin served a term as National President of the Institute of Embalmers. He served also from 1968 as a member of Leeds City Council and was accorded the honour of being Lord Mayor of Leeds in 1983. He was, and still is, one of the youngest Lord Mayors that Leeds has ever had. Martin relinquished active association with the company in 1985 and thereafter, the traditions and standards so long established are maintained to the present day by the current staff, and is without parallel in the city of Leeds. Although the company is not actually run by the Dodgson family nowadays, Martin still keeps an active interest in its progress into the millennium.

Above: Mr Martin Dodgson, youngest Lord Mayor of Leeds, wearing his mayoral chain of office.

Right: Martin's father, William, driving a hearse in the 1930s.

Above, right: An invoice, dating from 1913.

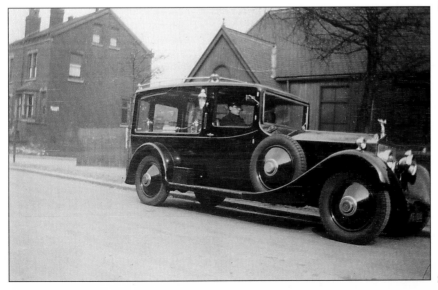

Wm Dodgson & Son

Funeral Directors

Lupton Avenue, Leeds,

West Yorkshire LS9 6EQ

Tel: 0113 249 8849
Fax: 0113 235 0084

Joseph Priestley: A scientific pioneer who was born in the West Riding.

Joseph Priestley is remembered chiefly for his scientific achievements. He was a pioneer in the chemistry of gases and the "discoverer" of oxygen. Born at Fieldhead in the parish of Birstall in 1733, he was the eldest of six children. His parents came from very typical eighteenth century West Riding backgrounds, his father being a maker and dresser of woollen cloth and his mother from an agricultural family.

Following the death of his mother when he was only six years old, Joseph Priestley was raised by his aunt and uncle. Their guardianship had a profound effect on Priestley, instilling strongly religious, Calvinist beliefs. Priestley had a comparatively good education for his time. Indeed, by the age of nineteen, few young men could boast proficiency in Latin, Greek and Hebrew; familiarity with Chaldee, Syriac and Arabic along with modem languages, Maths and Physics.

Priestley's interest in the sciences began in childhood. It was not uncommon for his family to find him experimenting, for example to see how long spiders could survive in a limited volume of air! After completing four years at a Dissenting Academy at Daventry, Northamptonshire, Priestley was ready to became a non-conformist minister. His first appointment was at Needham Market, Suffolk where he spent three disastrous years. His congregation dwindled owing to his "unsound" doctrine although he believed it to be his hereditary speech impediment. After only three years at Needham Market, Priestley took up a new ministry

at Nantwich in Cheshire where he found a more receptive congregation.

During his Nantwich ministry Priestley set up a school for thirty boys and six girls. Naturally science featured in the curriculum and such instruments as a small air pump and an electrical machine were among his early acquisitions. His friends and the parents of his scholars were frequently entertained by experiments using such equipment.

In September 1761 Joseph Priestley took up a teaching position at Warrington Academy. This institution was one of the few of its time which provided a more modern rather than traditional education. Priestley was engaged to teach languages and literature. Whilst spending his vacations in London, Priestley met a number of men such as Dr Benjamin Franklin who shared his enthusiasm for science. Franklin spent a great deal of time assisting Priestley with his book, "The History and Present State of Electricity" (published in 1766). Priestley's knowledge and enthusiasm so impressed his new friends that he was elected Fellow of the Royal Society, the most famous scientific body in the world.

In 1767 Priestley returned to Leeds to become minister of Mill Hill Chapel in City Square and then moved on to Calne in Wiltshire in 1773 as Librarian to Lord Shelbourne, a former Secretary of State. Here he continued his scientific experiments for which he was awarded the "Copley Medal" by the Royal Society.

From Wiltshire Priestley moved on to Birmingham in 1780. Toward the end of 1789 he, like many dissenters at that time, was branded a dangerous enemy of King and Country owing to his support of the repeal of the Test and Corporation Acts. When violence broke out in Birmingham during the summer of 1791, Priestley was one of the main targets sought by the mob. Fortunately he and his family managed to escape but his house, laboratory and chapel were completely destroyed.

On 7 April 1794 Joseph Priestley and his wife set sail for America. Within ten years Priestley died, on 6 February 1804.

Joseph Priestley College: 40 Years of Service in South Leeds

The beginnings of the Joseph Priestley College

In 1955 the West Riding established Area Institutes by amalgamation of existing Evening Institutes. Joseph Priestley Institute of Further Education was formed at that time and was so named because Batley and Birstall - his birthplace- was then in the area. Between 1955-73 the school contained six full-time academic staff plus Principal and five Heads of Centre. All teaching was done by part-time staff.

In the latter part of 1974 and the early part of 1975 the curriculum covered almost all part-time evening courses - Office Skills, GCEs, Crafts/Practical, Arts/Languages & Physical Education and between then and the early 1990s has developed to include full-time courses for school leavers and others. - Office Skills, Secretarial, Business & Finance, Computing, Special Needs, and General Education.

Due to the Education Reform Act of 1988 the College gained formal recognition as one of nine Further Education Colleges in Leeds. It elected a new Governing body and changed its name from Institute to College.

In April 1993, the College became independent from the Local Education Authority. Since Incorporation the College has grown by in excess of 60%. Joseph Priestley College celebrated its 40th birthday in 1995 with an 18th century party staged at its Peel Street Centre.

The College continues to receive gas bills and American Express card offers addressed to Joseph Priestley himself. It seems that news of the scientists death in 1804 has yet to spread to our utilities and mailing lists!

Students at the College are drawn from a wide range of ages and backgrounds. The college has also paid host to many overseas students. It is highly regarded for its work with students with learning difficulties and/or disabilities and was awarded a Grade 1, the highest attainable, for this curriculum area by the Government's Inspectorate in 1995. The College is open 7 days a week and offers provision during daytimes, evenings and weekends at its four Centres throughout South Leeds.

Left: The Joseph Priestley College Elmfield Centre at Bridge Street, Morley.
Above: The College's Alec Beevers Centre on Burton Avenue in Beeston.

Why should we be your first choice?

- **A wide range of courses**
- **Up to date facilities**
- **Flexible learning times -**

  Day, Evening and Weekends

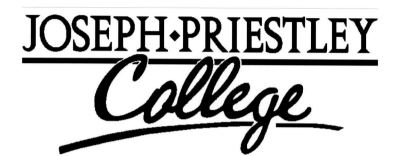
JOSEPH·PRIESTLEY College

- **Welcoming friendly environment**
- **Individual advice and help**
- **Local, accessible College**

  Centres throughout South Leeds

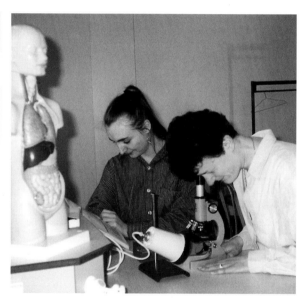

Over 10,000 adults and young people acquire new skills with us every year - why not join them?

Call the College Helpline on 0113 253 2244
or write to Joseph Priestley College
Freepost LS6408, Morley, Leeds, West Yorkshire, LS27 8YY.

Joseph Priestley College is committed to providing accessible education and training in and around South Leeds

Memories of Leeds

Harold Newsome: 60 years of building on great traditions

Harold Newsome Ltd was established in 1937, initially as a farrier's concern. Harold Newsome was a Master Farrier. This was during the era just before the massive use of motor transportation came to the fore. Eventually, with the complete phasing out of horses as transport the company began to specialise in small contract steelwork. Harold found a plot of land on Elder Road in Bramley, which originally was an old Tannery. Harold Newsome Ltd have been on the same site ever since. The original cranes were hand operated with ropes, and steel was pushed on a hand cart from railway sidings. Harold Newsome had two sons, Peter and Geoffrey who joined the company just after the war. Geoff was in the mining industry and Peter an RAF officer who, after being demobbed, began to develop the steel structure business with Geoff.

Nowadays, the company remains in family hands, in its third generation. Grandsons of the founder, Paul and Clive, Peter's sons, are joint managing directors.

Paul joined the company on leaving school as a lowly apprentice, starting from the bottom and working his way up. Clive joined later, in 1979, as manager. In the early 1980s, on Peter's death, both of his sons took over the business and continued to develop the structural steel side of the business, incorporating state-of-the-art CAD systems and high tech equipment, producing steel framed buildings which are second to none. The site was refurbished in 1980 and a new extension was added. The company works with most major contractors in the UK and carry out the erection of steel frame buildings throughout the country.

The company has developed steadily since its humble beginnings and has incorporated all the modern techniques of computer aided design and detailing etc. Harold Newsome Ltd is now celebrating its 60th year and will continue to progress as new new techniques are introduced.

Full in-house design facilities means that the company is extremely competitive and most of their work is carried out through repeat orders and word of mouth which signifies the quality of the work and customer satisfaction.

LOWE ENGINEERING

The Company started in the mid 1930s giving a service to the petroleum industry and supplying storage tanks, pipelines and reconditioned pumps. In the 1940s, through the needs of war, the Company started welding and machining in steel and aluminium and from these beginnings progressed through the years and successfully marketed its own products.

The 1960s saw collaboration with C.E.G.B. Scientific Services in the joint development of probes; special high performance heat exchangers; coolers and specialised sampling components for the power station boilers.

The 1980s saw the start of the new factory, which was completed in three phases, in order to cope with the successful worldwide exporting business, with main markets being India; Hong Kong; China and Africa. LOWE is now internationally recognised as a leading authority in the design and manufacture of sample conditioning systems for boiler water, steam, process liquids and gases in both power plant and process plant applications. More recently, Lowe have moved into supply of complete chemical monitoring analyser houses for many different applications including environmental monitoring for such as combustion emissions and waste water. Often including a full complement of process analysers, annunciators and recorders, with fully integrated heating, ventilation and lighting systems, together with data acquisition and transmission equipment.

The second specific area of expertise is that of high quality fabrication in aluminium alloys and stainless steels. These are supplied primarily to the industrial, marine and petrochemical markets for applications requiring high standards of workmanship to codes such as Lloyds; M.O.D.; A.S.M.E. Skilled and coded welders using qualified weld procedures are used on the construction of pressure and storage vessels for liquids such as nitroglycerine and nitric acid: recompression chambers for divers and marine fabrications from wheelhouses to complete workboats designed and built to customers requirements.

The Company received registration, by B.S.I. as far back as 1987, to the prestigious BS 5750 PART I which covers design, manufacture and installation and was one of the first smaller Companies to achieve this.

A vigorous management team ensures that customers will receive professional treatment and at the same time, continue to expand and develop the company along lines which will capitalise on the established strengths and skills of this small, but efficient Organisation.

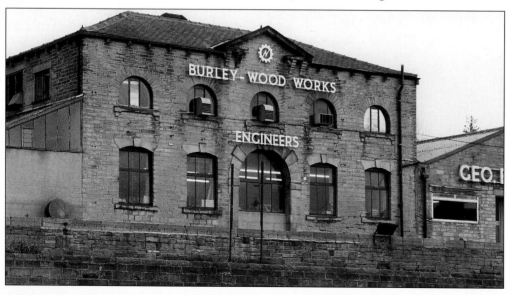

Above: A 1960s Bedford Cement tanker.
Left: George Lowe's Burley Wood Works.

Typical boiler installation - circa 1930

Traditional Values of Customer Service and Satisfaction

The tradition continues

The Company was founded by Herbert Morfitt around the turn of the century. He was a plumber operating in Headingley with a handcart, and his workshop was originally in a basement room under the Original Oak public house.

The business expanded in the early 1920s when Herbert's son, Geoffrey, joined his father to take the business forward, capitalising on the advent of central heating, and eventually the Company of H. Morfitt & Son Ltd. was formed on 3rd August 1939. It was about that time that the Company moved to their current premises in St. Michael's Lane.

Despite the depression years, the Company had made tremendous strides forward and had begun to build a reputation of customer service and satisfaction.

Following the war years, the Company continued to develop into a multi-discipline provider of heating, ventilation and plumbing services. In 1976 the Company was acquired by J. H. Shouksmith & Sons Ltd., a York-based family concern with a pedigree in the Plumbing Industry which can be traced back to their formation in 1820s.

Part of the Morfitt tradition through the majority of the life of the Company has been to train apprentices. Even in the recent years of recession the Company has continued to train young people for work in the Heating and Plumbing Industry. The Morfitt Medal for Plumbing Excellence has long been established as a much sought-after achievement at the Leeds College of Building Awards Ceremony.

Today as the tradition continues the Company contributes strongly to the Construction Industry, particularly in the Yorkshire area, whilst giving employment to 55 people. Through its fully computerised design and drawing facilities Morfitts endeavours to maintain its tradition of customer satisfaction whilst operating at the forefront of technology."

Artist: Andy Gilmour

The World Famous
CITY VARIETIES
MUSIC HALL

Home of BBC TV's

The Good Old Days

Management - Tel: **0113 242 5045**
Box Office - Tel: **0113 243 0808**

Swan Street, (off Briggate), Leeds
West Yorkshire LS1 6LW